Rain
Forest
Animals

by **Sharon Gordon**

Reading Consultant: Nanci R. Vargus, Ed.D.

Marshall Cavendish
Benchmark
New York

Picture Words

 anteater

 ants

 butterfly

 leaf

 orangutan

 parrots

 rain forest

 sloth

 snake

 tree

 tree frog

 trees

See the animals in the .

4

See the rest in the water.

See the hunt for .

See the fly
to a .

See the swing in the .

See the 🐸 sit on
a 🍃.

See the eat fruit.

See the hang from a .

 animals see me!

Words to Know

fruit (froot)
>   the part of a plant that can
>   be eaten

rain forest (rain FOR-ehst)
>   a thick forest where it rains
>   all year round

swing to move back and forth

Find Out More

Books

Doering, Amanda. *Rain Forest ABC: An Alphabet Book.* Mankato, MN: A+ Books, 2004.

Kratter, Paul. *The Living Rain Forest: An Animal Alphabet.* Watertown, MA: Charlesbridge Publishing, 2006.

Videos

Ecosystems for Children: All About Forest Ecosystems. Schlessinger Media, A Division of Library Video Company, 2006.

Really Wild Animals: Totally Tropical Rain Forest. National Geographic Society, 2005.

Web Sites

The Living Rainforest
www.livingrainforest.org/for/kids

Learning About Rainforests
www.srl.caltech.edu/personnel/krubal/rainforest/serve_home.html

Tropical Rainforest Information for Kids
kids.mongabay.com

About the Author

Sharon Gordon is an author, editor, and advertising copywriter. She is a graduate of Montclair State University in New Jersey and has written more than one hundred children's books, many for Marshall Cavendish, which include works of fiction, nonfiction, and cultural history. Along with her family, she enjoys exploring the plants and animals of the Outer Banks of North Carolina.

About the Reading Consultant

Nanci R. Vargus, Ed.D., wants all children to enjoy reading. She used to teach first grade. Now she works at the University of Indianapolis. Nanci helps young people become teachers. While in Australia, she explored the rain forest from a white-water raft and a sky tram.

Marshall Cavendish Benchmark
99 White Plains Road
Tarrytown, NY 10591-5502
www.marshallcavendish.us

Library of Congress Cataloging-in-Publication Data
Gordon, Sharon.
 Rain forest animals / by Sharon Gordon.
      p. cm. — (Benchmark Rebus. Animals in the wild)
Summary: "Easy to read text with rebuses explores animals that live in the rain forest"—Provided by publisher.
Includes bibliographical references.
ISBN 978-0-7614-2899-2
Rain forest animals—Juvenile literature. I. Title.
QL112.G67 2008
591.734—dc22
      2007041737

Editor: Christine Florie
Publisher: Michelle Bisson
Art Director: Anahid Hamparian
Series Designer: Virginia Pope

Photo research by Connie Gardner

Rebus images, with the exception of anteater, provided courtesy of *Dorling Kindersley.*

Cover photo by BIOS Klein and Hubert/Peter Arnold, Inc.

The photographs in this book are used with permission and through the courtesy of:
Corbis: Theo Allofs, 3 (anteater); Staffan Widstrand, 5; Tom Brakefield, 9; Envision, 11; *Getty Images*: Ed George, 7; *Dembinsky Photo Associates*: Anup Shah, 13; Fritz Polking, 17; *Minden Pictures*: Michael and Patricia Fogden, 15, 19; *age footstock*: Mark Jones, 21.

Printed in Malaysia
1 3 5 6 4 2